The T

D1644481

A Shakespeare Story

RETOLD BY ANDREW MATTHEWS
ILLUSTRATED BY TONY ROSS

ORCHARD

For Bob, Gill, Miriam and David
A.M.

For Jade and Siân
T.R.

ORCHARD BOOKS
338 Euston Road, London NW1 3BH
Orchard Books Australia
Hachette Children's Books
Level 17/207 Kent St, Sydney, NSW 2000
This text was first published in Great Britain in the form of a gift collection
called The Orchard Book of Shakespeare Stories, illustrated by
Angela Barrett in 2001.
This edition first published in hardback in Great Britain in 2002
First paperback publication in 2003
This slipcase edition published in 2013
Not for individual resale
Text © Andrew Matthews 2001
Illustrations © Tony Ross 2002
ISBN 978 1 40780 988 5
The rights of Andrew Matthews to be identified as the author and Tony Ross as
the illustrator of this work have been asserted by them in accordance with the
Copyright, Designs and Patents Act, 1988
A CIP catalogue record for this book is available from the British Library
Printed in China

Orchard Books is a division of Hachette Childrens Books,
an Hachette UK company.
www.hachette.co.uk

Contents

Cast List

Prospero
A wizard
The rightful Duke of Milan

Miranda

Daughter to Prospero

Caliban

Servant to Prospero

Ariel

An airy spirit

Antonio

Duke of Milan
Brother to Prospero

Alonso

King of Naples

Prince Ferdinand

Son to the King of Naples

Trinculo and Stephano

Sailors

The Scene

Mediterranean island in the fifteenth century.

O, I have suffered
With those that I saw suffer! A brave vessel,
Who had, no doubt, some noble creature in her,
Dashed all to pieces!

Miranda; I.iii.

The Tempest

A violent storm was raging over the
island. Palm trees bent and swayed like
dancers in the howling gale that tore off
their branches and sent them tumbling
through the air.

On a beach not far from the mouth of his cave, stood Prospero the wizard, his white hair and beard streaming out in the wind, his black robes flapping around him. As he

raised his left hand, thunder rumbled; he lifted the staff in his right hand, and forked lightning crackled, flickering like snakes' tongues across the inky clouds.

Out to sea,
a ship with
broken masts
and tattered
sails wallowed
helplessly as the
storm drove it

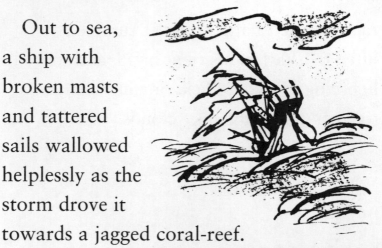

towards a jagged coral-reef.

A lovely young woman in a white gown
hurried out of the cave
and ran towards
Prospero, her
dark hair
whipping about
her face. She
caught the
wizard by the
sleeve and called
out, "Father!"

Prospero seemed not to hear her. His eyes burned silver with magic, and they stayed firmly fixed on the ship.

"Father!" shouted the young woman. "What are you doing? Everyone aboard that ship will be killed!"

Above the sound of the wind came a groaning crash of timber striking rock. A huge wave reared up like a startled horse and thundered down on the ship, making it vanish from sight.

Prospero lowered his hands. The wind dropped to a gentle breeze, the boiling clouds faded into a blue sky and the sun glinted on a calm sea.

"No one has been harmed, Miranda," said Prospero. "Everything is as I planned. For your sake, I have used my magic to help right a great wrong, done long ago."

"What wrong, Father?" Miranda asked with a puzzled frown.

"Enough!" said Prospero. He moved his left hand in front of Miranda's face, and she fell into an enchanted sleep where she stood.

Prospero took two paces towards the sea, looking out at the place where the ship had sunk. "Soon, my brother!" he whispered.

A sound made him turn his head in time to see a strange creature creeping up behind Miranda. It was shaped like a man, but its skin was covered with glistening green scales, and its eyes were as yellow as a lizard's.

"Caliban!"
Prospero said
sternly. "You
brought no
wood or water
to the cave this
morning. Must
I send the spirits
to torment you
again?"

Caliban scowled.
"I was not born to be
your servant!" he answered defiantly.
"My mother, the great witch Sycorax,
promised me that I would rule this
island, and so I would have – if you
had not come here, and stolen her books
of magic, and freed her slave-spirits to
help you drive her away!"

"Silence!" said Prospero, and he snapped his fingers.

Needles of fire seemed to lance through Caliban, forcing him to his knees. "Mercy, master, mercy!" he cried, bowing his head. The pain left him, and he hid his face so that Prospero could not see his cunning smile. "Why are you so cruel?" he whimpered. "You were kind to me once!"

"And you repaid my kindness by trying to kidnap my daughter!" snapped Prospero. "Get to work, you treacherous wretch!"

Caliban stood, and shambled off. "I will be revenged, one day!" he muttered to himself. "I will be King of this island, and I will take Miranda as my Queen!"

When Caliban was safely out of sight, Prospero lifted his staff. "Ariel!" he called softly. "Appear to me now, sweet spirit!"

There was a faint sound of music. Lights sparkled in the air, winking like sunshine on bursting bubbles. In the midst of the lights fluttered a young boy, with golden skin and white wings on his heels. He smiled at Prospero, and darted playfully around his head.

Prospero laughed. "Faithful Ariel!" he said. "Are the sailors scattered over the island as I commanded?"

"They are, good master," said Ariel, his voice like the gentle humming of a harp.

"And where is Ferdinand, the King of Naples' son?" Prospero demanded.

"Close by," said Ariel. "He mourns his father, believing him to be drowned."

"He is not drowned," said Prospero. "He wanders the island lost, with my brother Antonio." Prospero sighed, and old memories gave his face a far off look. "Twelve years ago, when I was Duke of Milan, my wife died," he said

sadly. "Grief blinded me to the treachery of Antonio, who plotted in secret with my old enemy, King Alonso of Naples. They overthrew me, and Antonio took my place.

I was put in an
open boat with
my daughter,
and cast adrift
to die. But
destiny took me
to this island, to
Sycorax's magic books, and
you. My spells brought the ship here, and
now it is time for mischief and magic."

"And revenge, master?" said Ariel.

Prospero shook
his head. "I do not
seek revenge, only
justice," he said.
"Go to Prince
Ferdinand
and bring
him here!"

Ariel's eyes darkened into doubt. "Will it be as thou promised, master? When thy plan is done, shall I be free?"

"Free as the wind, my Ariel," said Prospero. "I will break my spells, and no magic will ever hold you again."

Ariel glowed brightly, and flew off faster than Prospero's eyes could follow.

* * *

Prince Ferdinand was seated cross-legged on the sand. Salt water and the sun had bleached his brown hair almost blond, and his handsome face was lined with sadness.

Whenever he closed his eyes, he saw the massive waves that had swallowed the ship and cast him up on this uncharted island. He might never be found, and he wondered if it would be better to swim out to sea and join his drowned father than face a life of miserable loneliness...

His thoughts were suddenly interrupted
by lights dancing in front of his face,
swarming like bees.

They were so fascinating that Ferdinand could do nothing but stare at them. Then he heard music, and the singing of a sweet, high voice.

"Forget thy father, deep he lies,
With shining pearls set in his eyes.
Come with me now, Prince Ferdinand
And walk along the yellow sand!"

Ferdinand seemed to be caught up in a dream. Without a word he stood, and followed where the lights led him.

Prospero saw Ferdinand from afar,
following bewitched behind Ariel's
glimmering lights. When the young Prince
was close by, Prospero touched Miranda
on the shoulder, releasing her from the
spell. Instantly, she woke, and the first
thing she saw was Ferdinand. "Is this a
spirit, Father?" she gasped.

"No, my child. It is a man of flesh and blood like you and me," Prospero told her.

"But I thought all men had white hair and beards, like yours!" Miranda exclaimed.

Prospero smiled, and signalled to Ariel. The dancing lights vanished, and Ferdinand's trance was broken. He saw Miranda, and his eyes filled with wonder at her beauty. "Am I still dreaming?" he whispered. "Is this a vision?"

"I am no vision, sir," Miranda said. "I am as real as you are...if you are indeed real." Shyly, she reached out her hand. Ferdinand reached out his, and their fingertips touched.

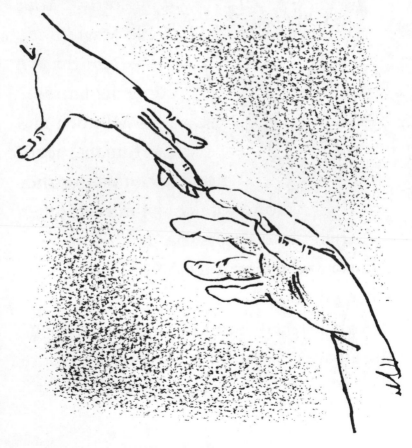

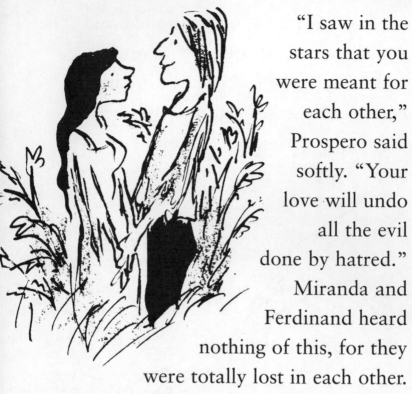

"I saw in the stars that you were meant for each other," Prospero said softly. "Your love will undo all the evil done by hatred." Miranda and Ferdinand heard nothing of this, for they were totally lost in each other.

"Ariel!" said Prospero. "Find King Alonso and my brother Antonio, and when you do..."

Ariel listened carefully, and before long the air was bright with his laughter.

On another part of the beach, two sailors
swayed across the sand, leaning against
each other to stop themselves
from falling over. One was Trinculo, a
thin man with ginger hair and a freckled
face, and his companion was Stephano,
who had a shock of grey hair and a
stomach as round as a watermelon.

They had been washed ashore together
with a cask of wine, which they had fast
consumed. Now they were so drunk, that
when Caliban jumped out from behind a
rock and grovelled at their feet, they were
not entirely sure that he was really there.

Caliban had been watching Trinculo and Stephano for some time, and his quick, cunning mind had seen a way to use them to get rid of his master, Prospero.

"Gentle Gods!" Caliban cried. "Have you come from the sky to save me?"

"He thinks we're Gods!" Trinculo giggled.

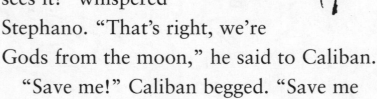

"Hmm, he's an ugly brute, but he knows good breeding when he sees it!" whispered Stephano. "That's right, we're Gods from the moon," he said to Caliban.

"Save me!" Caliban begged. "Save me

from the wicked enchanter who has enslaved me, and I will give you all his treasure and be your faithful servant forever!"

"Enchanter?" yelped Trinculo, turning pale.

"Courage, Trinculo!" Stephano murmured. "And what kind of treasure might that be, good monster?"

"Gold," said Caliban. "And silver. And many jewels."

Stephano drew his cutlass and waved it so clumsily that he almost cut off his right ear. "Pirates, enchanters – it's all the same to me!" he boasted. "Take me to the villain! I'll carve him into thin slices!"

With a whoop of delight, Caliban led
the way along the jungle track to
Prospero's cave.

After the long walk through the
jungle's heat, and shadows, and strange
sounds, Stephano's head began to clear
and he no longer felt as bold as he had
earlier, and Trinculo was trembling like a
mouse's whiskers.

"Er, is it much further?" Stephano asked Caliban.

"There!" Caliban replied, pointing.

Trinculo stood on tiptoes and peered. He could see the mouth of a cave, filled with an ominous darkness.

"Why d-don't we walk s-side by s-side?" he jibbered. "Then n-nothing can harm us!"

Even as he spoke, the darkness in the cave began to move. It poured out of the cave-mouth, coiling like black mist – and the mist transformed itself into a pack of savage black dogs, with red eyes and

slavering fangs. Snapping and snarling, the dogs bounded towards the intruders.

Trinculo and Stephano turned and ran screaming into the jungle, with Caliban close behind.

* * *

King Alonso and Antonio had also been wandering through the jungle for hours, and now they were desperate with thirst and hunger. Their fine clothes, ripped by cruel thorns, hung round them in tatters, and sweat streamed down their faces. Alonso, certain that Ferdinand was dead, was stricken with grief, and at last he slumped on to the trunk of a fallen tree.

"I can go no further!" he groaned. "I will wait here for death to put an end to my misery!"

Antonio glanced around uneasily. The jungle was an eerie place, full of shadows and whispering voices. "Just a little further, my lord!" he said. "I see a clearing not far ahead. Perhaps we will find a spring of fresh water there." The thought of water urged Alonso to his feet and together the two men stumbled towards the edge of the clearing.

Like a mirage, in the middle of the clearing stood a long table, piled with food and drink – golden platters of carved meats, whole roasted fowl, baskets of bread and golden jugs of wine.

Alonso and Antonio hurried towards it,
but before they could reach the feast, there
was a dazzling flash of light and Ariel
appeared. He hovered over the table in the
shape of a harpy – a monster with a human

head and the body of a gigantic eagle.
Alonso tried to snatch a jug of wine, but
the harpy hissed and slashed at him with its
bronze talons.

"Foul spirit, why do you torment us?"
Antonio sobbed.

"For thy betrayal of thy brother
Prospero and niece Miranda!" the harpy
screeched. "Thou and King Alonso did set
them in a boat and leave them to the
mercy of the ocean. Prepare thee for thy
punishment!"

Alonso and Antonio stared in amazement, wondering how the spirit had discovered their guilty secret. They expected the harpy to tear them into pieces, but instead it faded into a cloud of tiny lights that swirled like specks of dust floating in a beam of sunlight. The two men felt themselves fall into a waking sleep, and heard a voice speaking to them out of the cloud. "Come!" it said. "Follow, follow!"

From all over the island, the crew of the wrecked ship came to gather on the beach near Prospero's cave, drawn there by magic – even Trinculo and Stephano, who had aching heads and torn clothes from

where the hounds had snapped at them. The sailors rejoiced to see friends they thought had perished, and gazed about in wonder. Had the storm only been a dream, or were they dreaming now?

For there was their ship, undamaged, anchored close to the shore. The sailors laughed, and scratched their heads, unable to believe their luck.

Ariel brought Alonso and Antonio to the mouth of Prospero's cave, and broke their trance. Alonso gasped as Ferdinand and Miranda stepped out of the darkness, hand in hand, and his eyes blurred with tears. "What wonderful new world is this that has such people in it?" he wondered.

"The world that will be made when we return to Naples and our children are joined in marriage," said a voice.

Alonso and Antonio turned, and saw Prospero standing behind them. Antonio could not meet his brother's eyes, and hung his head in shame.

"Let our old hate be ended by their young love, Alonso," Prospero said. He came forward, and placed his hand on Antonio's shoulder. "I forgive you, brother," he said. "We will rule Milan together and end our days in peace. Now, go down to the shore and make ready to leave this island forever."

"Are you coming, Father?" asked Miranda.

"In a moment, my child," Prospero said. He waited until he was alone, then whispered, "Ariel?"

Ariel grew out of emptiness. Too excited to hold one shape, he turned into a humming bird,

then a butterfly,

then a winged unicorn.

"I have burned my books of magic and my wizard's staff," Prospero declared. "You are free to go, my Ariel, but I shall sadly miss you!"

"And I shall miss thee, dear master!" said Ariel. "But look for me in springtime blossom, or when the summer breeze stirs thy curtain, or when the winter stars blaze bright. Until then, farewell!"

"Farewell, sweet spirit!" said Prospero, and he turned away so that Ariel would not see the tears in his eyes.

✳ ✳ ✳

As the ship's sails unfurled and it began to glide away, Caliban came out of his hiding place in the jungle. He danced on the beach, turning cartwheels as he whooped, "I am King of the island! King!"

His voice frightened a flock of parrots who clattered out of the treetops and flew over Caliban in a great circle, their plumage glittering like the jewels in a royal crown.

Our revels now are ended. These our actors,
As I foretold you, were all spirits, and
Are melted into air, into thin air;

Prospero; IV.i.

Power in the Tempest

When we first meet Prospero, using magic to raise a storm and wreck a ship, he seems to be an evil magician. Prospero has enslaved the spirit, Ariel, and is now master to the monster Caliban. He has the power of magic at his fingertips, and is in a position of power over the island.

Gradually we learn that Prospero is not as wicked as he appears. He was once Duke of Milan, but was overthrown by his brother, Antonio, and Alfonso, the King of Milan. Prospero and his little daughter, Miranda, were cast adrift in an open boat that brought them to the island. The ship that Prospero wrecks at the start of the play carries Antonio, his son Ferdinand, and King Alfonso. They and all the sailors are washed safely ashore.

Prospero knows that Ferdinand and Miranda are destined to love each other, and that their love will put right the great wrong that was done to him twelve years before. He does not seek revenge, but justice, and when it finally comes, Prospero uses his power wisely and mercifully. Old enemies are humbled, but not humiliated. Prospero sets Ariel free and leaves Caliban master of the island once more.

The Tempest is one of Shakespeare's last plays, and he died two years after writing it. Many people believe that in the scene where Prospero destroys his magician's staff and books of magic, he speaks for Shakespeare, who is saying goodbye to the magical world of the theatre.

Shakespeare and the Globe Theatre

Some of Shakespeare's most famous plays were first performed at the Globe Theatre, which was built on the South Bank of the River Thames in 1599.

Going to the Globe was a different experience from going to the theatre today. The building was roughly circular in shape, but with flat sides: a little like a doughnut crossed with a fifty-pence piece. Because the Globe was an open-air theatre, plays were only put on during daylight hours in spring and summer. People paid a penny to stand in the central space and watch a play, and this part of the audience became known as 'the groundlings' because they stood on the ground. A place in the tiers of seating beneath the thatched roof, where there was a slightly better view and less chance of being rained on, cost extra.

The Elizabethans did not bath very often and the audiences at the Globe were smelly. Fine ladies and gentlemen in the more expensive seats sniffed perfume and bags of sweetly-scented herbs to cover the stink rising from the groundlings.

There were no actresses on the stage; all the female characters in Shakespeare's plays would have been acted by boys, wearing wigs and make-up. Audiences were not well-behaved. People clapped and cheered when their favourite actors came on stage; bad actors were jeered at and sometimes pelted with whatever came to hand.

Most Londoners worked hard to make a living and in their precious free time they liked to be entertained. Shakespeare understood the magic of the theatre so well that today, almost four hundred years after his death, his plays still cast a spell over the thousands of people that go to see them.

Orchard Classics
Shakespeare Stories

Retold by Andrew Matthews
Illustrated by Tony Ross

Orchard Books are available from all good bookshops.